What Is American in American Art

What Is American in American Art

Introduction by Lloyd Goodrich
Catalogue by Mary Black

 Clarkson N. Potter, Inc./Publisher NEW YORK
DISTRIBUTED BY CROWN PUBLISHERS, INC.

Frontispiece: 104. *The Bootleggers*, by Thomas Hart Benton

For a long time Americans who cared about culture were preoccupied with the stature of our native art—or, more exactly, how it compared with European art. Within the past three decades, however, this aesthetic introspection has shifted, and we have begun to think more about the nature than the stature of the home product.

Writing in the wake of the 1938 exhibition of three centuries of American art that was organized for export to Paris by The Museum of Modern Art, Edward Alden Jewell published a collection of essays called *Have We An American Art?* About twenty-five years later, when they issued their memorable collection of related studies, Jean Lipman and the editors of "Art in America" put the question as *What Is American in American Art?*

Of course, the rise of the New York school within the international art scene had much to do with this growth of self-confidence. I think that it can also be traced to the serious study and identification of our self-taught painters and sculptors and the emergence of a New York City museum concerned exclusively with American folk art.

It is surely noteworthy that M. Knoedler & Company has focused on American painting to inaugurate the opening of its new gallery. But, in a sense, that choice was heralded as early as 1852, when Michel Knoedler commissioned George Caleb Bingham's "Canvassing for Votes." It is probably more significant that the paintings brought together now under the Knoedler auspices have been selected by Mary Black, who is a folk art specialist, and assembled in honor of Joseph B. Martinson, the founder of the Museum of American Folk Art. I cannot help noting with some satisfaction that almost one third of the works included are folk art masterpieces. And I believe it is largely on their account that *What Is American in American Art* can be presented in 1971 as an assertion rather than as a question.

M. J. Gladstone
Director, Museum of American Folk Art

Lenders to the Exhibition

Addison Gallery of American Art, Andover, Mass.

Albany Institute of History and Art, Albany, N.Y.

Miss Mary Allis, Fairfield, Conn.

Mr. and Mrs. Lee Ault, N.Y.C.

Baltimore Museum of Art, Baltimore, Md.

Boston Athenaeum, Boston, Mass.

Mr. Anthony Bower, N.Y.C.

Mr. Edward A. Bragaline, N.Y.C.

Carnegie Institute, Museum of Art, Pittsburgh, Pa.

Cedar Rapids Art Center, Cedar Rapids, Iowa

Century Club, N.Y.C.

Mrs. Stuart Davis, N.Y.C.

Mr. Oliver Eldridge, Canaan, Conn.

Everson Museum of Art, Syracuse, N.Y.

Mr. Robert L. Fisher, Litchfield, Conn.

Col. and Mrs. Edgar W. Garbisch, N.Y.C.

Graham Galleries, N.Y.C.

Mr. Herbert W. Hemphill, Jr., N.Y.C.

Hirschl & Adler Galleries, N.Y.C.

Historical Society of Pennsylvania, Philadelphia, Pa.

James Jerome Hill Reference Library, St. Paul, Minn.

Mrs. Barbara E. Johnson, Princeton, N.J.

Mr. and Mrs. Alfred Winslow Jones, N.Y.C.

Mr. and Mrs. Jacob M. Kaplan, N.Y.C.

M. Knoedler & Co., N.Y.C.

Mr. and Mrs. Bertram K. Little, Brookline, Mass.

Mr. Tasker G. Lowndes, N.Y.C.

Mr. Dan W. Lufkin, N.Y.C.

Estate of Joseph B. Martinson

Metropolitan Museum of Art, N.Y.C.

Mr. and Mrs. J. William Middendorf II, N.Y.C.

Minneapolis Institute of Arts, Minneapolis, Minn.

Mr. and Mrs. Robert Montgomery, N.Y.C.

Museum of American Folk Art, N.Y.C.

Museum of the City of New York, N.Y.C.

Museum of Fine Arts, Boston, Mass.

Museum of Fine Arts, Springfield, Mass.

Museum of Modern Art, N.Y.C.

National Academy of Design, N.Y.C.

National Baseball Hall of Fame, Cooperstown, N.Y.

National Cowboy Hall of Fame, Oklahoma City, Okla.

National Gallery of Art, Washington, D.C.

Mr. and Mrs. Avon Neal, North Brookfield, Mass.

Mr. and Mrs. Roy Neuberger, N.Y.C.

Newark Museum, Newark, N.J.

New-York Historical Society, N.Y.C.

New York Public Library, N.Y.C.

New York State Historical Association, Cooperstown, N.Y.

New York University Art Collection, N.Y.C.

The Paine Art Center and Arboretum, Oshkosh, Wisc.

Pennsylvania Academy of Fine Arts, Philadelphia, Pa.

Redwood Library, Newport, R.I.

Abby Aldrich Rockefeller Folk Art Collection, Williamsburg, Va.

Mr. and Mrs. Samuel Schwartz, Paterson, N.J.

Shelburne Museum, Shelburne, Vt.

Sleepy Hollow Restorations, Tarrytown, N.Y.

Mr. and Mrs. George A. Stern, N.Y.C.

Vassar College Art Gallery, Poughkeepsie, N.Y.

Wadsworth Atheneum, Hartford, Conn.

Mr. John Hay Whitney, N.Y.C.

Whitney Museum of American Art, N.Y.C.

Worcester Art Museum, Worcester, Mass.

Yale University Art Gallery, New Haven, Conn.

Preface

by Mary Black

Early in the 19th century, deTocqueville, that ever practical observer of American life, summarized one aspect of our national character, "Americans," he wrote, "habitually prefer the useful to the beautiful, and they will require that the beautiful shall be useful." His epigram pinpoints a consideration which for two centuries separated the American idea of beauty in art from Europe's. Another divider can be discerned in the unselfconsciousness with which the American artist taught himself to solve the practical problems of representation.

Within fifty years of the Pilgrim landing, Puritans were recording other Puritans in flamboyant disregard of strictures against images and sumptuary laws alike. In another fifty years—and in the equally unlikely climate of Dutch New Amsterdam—American painting production began in earnest. This record of faces, acres cleared, religious observances and scenes of daily life by untutored artists served as the American model for the 18th century and formalized an American conception of beauty. Because the early painters were finding their own solutions and establishing new standards of taste for their patrons, form and composition tended to be broader and more individual than that seen on the continent and in England. Until Benjamin West began the exodus to Italy and England in the last half of the 18th century, the development of painters from the practitioners of other crafts was responsible for the skilled selection, preparation and application of materials, pigments and varnishes.

For the first 150 years painting in America was the vocation of mostly middle class painters: not until the late days of the Hudson River School could an American artist become rich solely through the pursuit of his art. This fact was one that impressed the earlier artists' work most profoundly. As a member of a majority class working for his peers, the painter's interest and intent was to recreate a picture of his world and the possessions or interests that its members wished to have recorded in a permanent way. Niagara Falls or Natural Bridge might draw his attention for several repeats on several yards of canvas but it was not until the time of Cole and Kensett and Durand that the fall of light on New World nature became the central concern of an entire artistic career.

From America's earliest years, the national characteristic most commented on by natives and travelers alike has been our assertive individuality. While the middle class American was inclined to rejoice in his society and in his limited but highly remarkable and individual world, visitors from abroad almost universally condemned the residents on this side of the water for their materialism and lack of gentility. The American

7

determination to celebrate solid achievement and the compulsion to settle, tame and sow the wild land is seen in many early portraits with landscape backgrounds like that of *Abraham Wendell* in which his visage and his possessions are both described.

Often the American experience was defined in its painting as efficiently as it was in its literature. Native writers quickly gave voice to a kind of early Christian simplicity. Jonathan Edwards exultantly saw "in almost everything God's excellence, his wisdom, his purity and love." The same point of view is manifest in a painting of a Dutch born New York gentlewoman, *Elsje Rutgers Vas* of Kingston. Edwards' "sweet hours . . . . . on the banks of Hudson's river" find an illustration in Pieter Vanderlyn's *Pau de Wandelaer.*

The painter who taught himself was grappling with his own experience—with his life and with his art. The need to produce a painting that was a reflection of life was balanced between what he saw and what others saw. This struggle between what one wished to do and what one *could* do resulted in a tautness and strength that was a uniquely American phenomenon. This intensity is seen in portraits like deaf John Brewster's *Sarah Prince* of Newburyport. One can envision the artist in James Russell Lowell's terms, as "everyman—conscious that he leads two lives, the one trivial and ordinary, the other sacred and recluse: one which he carries to society and the dinner table, the other in which his youth and aspiration survive."

Eventually the idea of a painter who found his own solutions gave way to the trained artist consciously seeking explicit means for illustrating the beauty of an American landscape. The two separate ways of capturing beauty glanced at each other but never collided, like ghosts scarcely conscious of other wraiths passing near. Thus Erastus Field painting on his inland island along the Connecticut might have looked up and seen Thomas Cole sketching the river's oxbow high on the opposite bank. While Cole would set Cooper's pioneers in paint, Fields' subjects might be illustrations of Washington Irving's "little retired valleys [in which] population, manners, and customs remain fixed, while the great torrent of migration and improvement sweeps by them unobserved. They are like little brooks of still water, which border a rapid stream, where we may see the straw and bubble riding quietly at anchor . . . . . undisturbed by the passing current."

The intense spiritual explorations that have always been part of American character were given aesthetic expression by self-taught country painters like Hicks, Erastus Field, William Prior and Joseph Hidley—each of them personally involved in the religious movements that were part of the American adventure. The elements involving symbolism and pursuit with which Melville endowed Ahab are oddly similar to the torment of spirit and mind that Edward Hicks visualized in more than half a hundred *Peaceable Kingdoms.* Yet in his pastoral explorations of Bucks County farms the same Hicks can illustrate de Crèvecoeur's desire "to examine how the world is gradually settled, how the howling swamp is converted into a pleasing meadow, the rough ridge into a fine field."

The romantic and material part of the world would find translators in Eakins and

Homer, who explored the beauty that lighted even commonplace incidents. Yankee simplicity, further refined by Shaker purity, had a lasting effect on American art. Its impress traced in the selection of the basic and essential in the painting of Charles Sheeler, even—with a touch of the elemental and gorgeous added—to that of Georgia O'Keeffe. All turned back to Thoreau's psalm, "simplicity, simplicity . . . . let your affairs be as two or three . . . . and keep your accounts on your thumb nail."

The precision of the machine, its necessary exactness for performance adjusted, corrected and changed toward perfection became the subject for other painters. This jazzy beat of mind dance and machine come together in Stuart Davis' *American Emblem* and in Demuth's *Buildings, Lancaster*. Thomas Wolfe's loneliness and separateness in city streets is echoed in Hopper's *Sunday Morning* and George Tooker's *Subway*.

The subjects of this show are those that answer the question of its title in the most succinct and expressive terms. Sometimes the response is a bold rejoicing; just as often it is quiet, recalling Henry James' assertion "that the province of art is all life, all feeling, all observation, all vision." Because of limitations of size this exploration is confined to aesthetic expression as it expanded from the Atlantic seacoast westward, through the rise of mechanization and technology, and into the 20th century—when the question of what is most American in our art became nearly invalid as our national walls expanded to more than encircle the world.

Arbitrarily the beginning of this bare skeleton of what is American in our art was set on the first major production of painting in this country's history. The end is essentially the group outpouring of the American experience sponsored by WPA—although several of the artists represented had just begun to paint when WPA ended.

The theme, "What is American in American Art," comes from the book with the same title, edited by Jean Lipman and published by McGraw-Hill. The exhibition honors the memory of Joseph B. Martinson, the founder and chief supporter and champion of the Museum of American Folk Art in its first five years as a New York cultural institution.

I want to express my gratitude to the collectors, museum directors and curators whose cooperation and interest made this show possible, most especially to Myron J. Gladstone, director of the Museum of American Folk Art, and Anthony Bower of M. Knoedler & Co. for their valued assistance in organizing this exhibition and in editing its catalog.

Introduction

by Lloyd Goodrich

One of the most American traits is our urge to define what is American. This search for a self-image is a result of our relative youth as a civilization, our years of partial dependence on Europe. But it is also a vital part of the process of growth.

National characteristics in themselves have no absolute value. The intrinsic values of art lie in its universal and timeless elements. But national character has an importance like that of the individual artist's personality in relation to his art. Native elements in the art of a country contribute fundamentals, which can be modified by influences from other countries and other ages. So the problem is to define the elements in American art which are the products of our land and society and to consider how they have been affected by the art of the world.

"American" in what respect? In subject-matter, in viewpoint, in emotional and intellectual content, in artistic concepts, in style? Native subject-matter is obviously "American" by its very nature. More to the point is the question of artists' viewpoints toward their native subject-matter and what they make out of it. Emotional and intellectual content is a deeper factor. Artistic concepts, the degree of artistic naiveté or knowledge, involve relations to world art.

Art developed in America amid conditions such as existed in no European nation. Instead of a civilized society inhabiting the same regions for centuries, here was a group of colonies drawn from many countries. And for the first century and a half, conditions were unfavorable to the growth of any art. Up through the Revolution our people were too busy settling a continent and building a nation to have much time and energy for any but the most utilitarian arts. There was no centralized government, no royal court, no cultured nobility. The simple churches had no need for religious art, and in New England there was the Puritan aversion to images. Historical art requires official patronage and a long background of history. Classical themes would have seemed even more foreign, and would have involved the forbidden motif of the nude. Pictures of daily life were of no interest to the mercantile aristocracy. Though there were some landscape paintings of a naive kind, a people engaged in fighting the wilderness had little use for the romantic sentiment for nature.

Up to the end of the 18th century, the only kind of art which people of wealth and position considered necessary was portraiture; and it was in portraiture that American

33. *Lady with Birthmark*, by Isaac Sheffield

artists made their first achievements. It is a tribute to man's innate creativity that in such conditions so many portraits were produced which were also fine as art.

From the earliest days Americans possessed the great books of the world, but they owned no great art until the middle of the 19th century. In the absence of art schools, professional standards were represented by a few foreign-trained artists who were themselves not the most successful practitioners in their own countries; "dukes do not emigrate." Many native-born artists began as craftsmen—house, sign and carriage painters. Not until the last quarter of the 19th century were American art schools to approach European standards; until then many of our artists, including some of the best, were largely self-taught.

Hence early America had a larger proportion of folk art than Europe; and this remained true well into the 19th century. Created by innate talent directly out of local content, folk art contained the essence of native flavor on a popular level. This native flavor first appeared in a pure form in the limners who painted portraits in the colonies from the middle 17th century on. While varying from colony to colony, they had in common the primitive virtues—first-hand observation, integrity of form, and instinct for color, line and pattern—that belong to the primitive the world over.

The tragedy of primitive virtues is that they are doomed to disappear; their possessor aspires toward more conscious knowledge and skill, and in the process often loses more than he gains. Inevitably, Europe had a magnetic attraction for the American artist. Over there were the masterpieces, the ordered landscape humanized and mellowed by centuries of cultivation. By contrast America was crude, raw, an artistic desert. So the irresistible urge was toward closer contact with Europe. An essential factor in the growth of American art has been the interaction—sometimes the conflict—between native creativity and the powerful pull of European knowledge and skills. Some artists have matured through this interaction; some have been ruined by it; some have remained impervious.

Take the case of Copley. His art grew out of the colonial tradition. His American portraits had all the primitive virtues, plus a sculptural sense of form and an architectonic sense of design. But Copley aspired toward the sophistication of the fashionable British portraitists, was dissatisfied with provincial New England, and longed for the great world of Europe. After he settled in London his native style gave way to a more knowledgeable elegance, but without the primitive power of his American work. Thus America lost her greatest artist, to add another good painter to the British school. Copley's case illustrates clearly the typically American conflict between the innocent eye and the mind aspiring toward more knowledge.

As the United States emerged from colonialism into nationhood, our more intelligent artists were drawn increasingly to Europe. When, unlike Copley, they elected to return here, many of them strove to expand the range of native art beyond portraiture. It was in London, in Benjamin West's studio, that the first American attempts at the grand style originated—in West's own innovations, and his pupils'. From his studio Charles Willson Peale came home to paint his invaluable record of the Revolution and its leaders. While less gifted than Copley, Peale retained all his life a primitive strength of character and form, and became the foremost continuer of the colonial tradition.

But the problem of the imaginative artist in early 19th-century America is demonstrated by the example of Washington Allston. The most richly cultivated mind in our early art, steeped in Italy and the old masters, he spent seven years in London painting his finest works, which beneath their old-masterish stylisms revealed a wild romantic poetry. But after his return to America in middle age his art showed a progressive loss of vitality. An artist who needed contact with great art, in America he found none, nor any colleagues with anything like his knowledge. His case was the reverse of Copley's; with the latter, inborn realistic power was lost in acquiring European sophistication, while with Allston, romantic emotion and great intentions were starved by separation from Europe—the response of two opposite temperaments to the magnetism of Europe.

The defeat of Allston, and of his fellow aspirants toward the grand style, John Trumbull, John Vanderlyn and Samuel F. B. Morse, marked the end of the first noble attempt to break the yoke of portrait-painting, and to found an American school of great subject-matter.

Colonial limitations continued into the early decades of the 19th century. In the absence of governmental or ecclesiastical patronage, the chief support of art came from the upper middle class. This support determined the range and character of our art. Well into the century portraiture retained its predominance, and was the branch of our art marked by the most widely diffused professional skill, the greatest realistic strength, and on the whole the most substantial achievement. In spite of the deadly dullness of the run-of-the-mill product, the school included a surprising variety—from Ralph Earl, who went to England a primitive and came back a unique and captivating blend of naiveté and maturity, to the cosmopolitan elegance of Sully. In this heyday of American portraiture our artists achieved all degrees of balance between native character and worldly sophistication.

When national taste began to broaden in the 1820's and 1830's it was not in the direction of the neo-classic grand style but in more familiar fields. Westward expansion brought a realization of the vast scale and natural wonders of the continent. Increasing wealth was producing an urban bourgeoisie whose interest in art, though limited, went beyond the perpetuation of their own and their families' faces. Artists began to turn to native subjects, particularly in landscape and genre.

Some landscape had been produced since early days, but by folk artists or as the occasional recreation of portraitists. The first definite school of landscape appeared in the 1820's—the Hudson River school. The Hudson River painters formed a consciously native school, the first in our art. They were tremendously proud of America's natural beauties. In all simplicity they believed that the nobler the subject, the nobler the picture would be, and that the way to express nature's beauty was to represent her faithfully, leaf by leaf.

The artistic limitations of the school were obvious enough. Though contemporaries of the French Romantics and the Barbizon painters, they showed no awareness of the new trends; their romanticism took the form of literal representation of romantic subjects rather than expression of romantic ideas and emotions in the language of art. In relation to French art, their artistic concepts were anachronistic. But their direct contact with nature and skill of eye and hand had their own values. In their less pretentious pictures, and in the works of other native landscapists such as Lane and Heade, the character of our country, its spaciousness and solitude, the clearness of our air, the brilliance of our light, our high remote skies, were pictured truly and with a romantic emotion that is still alive.

The rise of genre painting was a product of the Jacksonian era's new sense of the importance of the common man. To the new generation the everyday life of the American people did not seem too vulgar for art. Soon our painters were covering many facets of that life: the humors and recreations of the old-fashioned Yankee farm, the hardy existence of the Western settlers. As was natural in a nation still largely agricultural, the favorite theme was country life. This nostalgia for the country was an essential element of the 19th-century American mind. The bourgeois, facing the new America of railroads and factories, looked back on the farm and childhood as a golden age. In artistic concepts and style, the genre painters were as *retardataire* in their relation to their European contemporaries as were our landscapists. But the best of them, such as Mount, Bingham, Blythe and Johnson, had virtues that were independent of current trends and that have made their work last. So until the middle of the 19th century, the greatest growth of American art had been in the discovery of native subject-matter rather than of new artistic concepts.

The first French movement to have a decided influence in America was the Barbizon school. In the 1850's several Americans visited Barbizon, particularly Inness, who was deeply affected by Corot, and Hunt, who became Millet's champion in America. The Barbizon influence was a liberating one, from literal representation toward subjective expression and a more painterly style. Inness revolutionized American landscape painting: instead of the cult of the wilderness, a preference for the pastoral and civilized; instead of grandiosity, a love of nature's intimate aspects; instead of nature as external phenomena, a sense of her as a being whose changing moods are shared by man.

The early work of Homer and Eakins was both a continuation of the native genre tradition and the beginning of something new—naturalism. In Europe, innovating artists were turning from classic or romantic subject-matter to the world around them, and painting it with a direct first-hand vision that disregarded traditional styles. But there is no evidence that either Homer or Eakins came under the influence of French naturalism or its leader, Courbet. Both of them had an unusually close relation to American actualities. More mature than their native predecessors, they were stronger in their realism, wider in range, deeper in content. Homer became the greatest 19th-century pictorial poet of outdoor America—the sea, the forest, the mountains, and the men who inhabited them. In his energy, the pristine freshness of his vision, and his simple sensuous vitality, he embodied the extrovert elements of the American spirit as no preceding artist had. Eakins, on the other hand, with uncompromising realism built his art out of the middle-class city life of his times, and created the most profound and revealing record of it. Our first mature artist to accept completely the realities of American urban life, he can be looked upon as the fulfiller of the native realistic tradition which Copley had first brought to full expression but had failed to continue.

Much the same relation as Homer's and Eakins' to native realism was that of Ryder to that other characteristic strain in the American mind, romanticism. While Ryder never painted a specifically "American" subject (except his early farm scenes) he was as typically American as Melville or Emily Dickinson. In his work all the dead wood of his romantic predecessors was eliminated. Concentrating on the inner reality of the mind's eye, he created the purest poetic imagery in our art of the 19th century.

Homer, Eakins and Ryder, like the earlier landscape and genre painters, lived most of their lives in America and built their art out of American life or the subjective life of the mind. They had little connection with current foreign movements—impressionism, neo-impressionism, post-impressionism—and in relation to them could be considered anachronistic. Yet, they were among the strongest creators in our history. This anomaly illustrates certain peculiarities in the development of 19th-century American art. Many of the most vital contributions were made by native artists with no relation to advanced trends abroad. American art so far was marked more by vigorous naturalistic representation or romantic personal expression, than by innovations in basic artistic concepts. Most such innovations originated abroad and were imported by artists more knowledgeable and impressionable, but generally less creative. Thus the evolution of our art in the 19th century can be seen in terms of two main forces: native creativity, often limited, but making its fundamental contribution, and international influences, contributing the leaven of knowledge and new concepts. Through the interaction of these two forces, American art of the 19th century evolved toward maturity.

Had there so far been characteristics that could be called "American"? It seems clear that there had been. In the naturalistic tradition represented by the colonial limners, Copley, the genre painters, and Homer and Eakins, there had been common elements: adherence to facts, directness of vision, clarity, solidity. With the Hudson River painters these stylistic qualities had been applied to romantic subject-matter. Among the subjective romanticists there had been common elements of dark color, subdued light, veiled outlines, the creation of a twilight or nocturnal world. Relationships, conscious or

84. *Hound and Hunter*, by Winslow Homer

unconscious, could be traced; in portraiture, the limners, Feke, Copley, the Peales, Earl, Neagle, Eakins; in landscape, Cole, Durand, Kensett, Cropsey, Lane, Heade, Inness, Martin; in genre, Mount, Bingham, Johnson, Homer, Eakins; in still-life, Raphaelle Peale, Harnett, Peto; in subjective romanticism, Allston, Page, Fuller, Newman, Ryder, Blakelock. And there was growth: Homer could be thought of as a more mature Mount, Eakins as a more profound Copley, Ryder as a more creative Allston.

The end of the Civil War introduced a new era of material expansion, with increased wealth and cosmopolitanism. For artists, European study became *de rigueur*. The growing internationalism of American art was shown by the fact that three leading Americans of the period, Whistler, Sargent and Cassatt, expatriated themselves.

On the other hand, there was a time-lag of ten to fifteen years in the arrival in America of French impressionism. Transplanted to our shores, impressionism was modified by native naturalism and sentiment to produce a variation that was distinctively American. The movement's emphasis on the outdoors, sunlight and the smiling aspects of nature, met a response in the optimistic spirit of a generation enjoying a new freedom in outdoor life, sports and summer vacations.

By the turn of the century, the American art world had become predominantly academic. The younger generation's foreign study had been mostly in the conservative schools of Paris. Returning home they combined American idealism, French impressionism, Whistlerian aesthetics, and Sargent's brushwork, to produce an academic art which was unmistakably and (with some honorable exceptions) deplorably "American." Preoccupied with the American Woman more than ever in our history, this art was yet strangely sexless. It showed no satire, or indeed any trace of humor. The city was seldom pictured, and the landscapists selected the idyllic in nature, shunning the man-made features that gave the face of modern America its character. This academic art, in spite of its cosmopolitan veneer, was as provincial as the 19th-century genre school, but without its raciness.

About 1905 the academic calm was invaded by a group of young realist painters centering around Robert Henri. Rebelling against sweetness and light, they turned to the teeming life of the modern city. Their humor, social conscience, and feeling for the urban masses were new notes in our painting. Their radicalism, however, lay in their subjects and viewpoint rather than in their style, at first no more advanced than pre-impressionist French painting. But their vital interest in contemporary American life started one of the dominant strains in 20th-century American art.

Almost simultaneously the European modern movements began to reach this country. Young American artists abroad had played a part in their beginnings; never before had so many Americans been involved so early in European movements. And modernism reached these shores earlier than any previous foreign development; within eight years of the birth of fauvism and five of that of cubism, the Armory Show presented a full panorama of the new art to a shocked but curious public.

Modernism was the most radical interruption so far to the provincial tendencies of American art. But as with previous movements, it became modified in America. In this country it was marked by comparatively few radical innovations. In Europe the innovators believed that the possibilities of representational art had been exhausted, and that the only path was a search for a new visual language. But our art was far from having reached that historic stage.

There was less experimentation with basic artistic concepts than in Europe. Cubism had only a few exponents, none of them orthodox. But it had a much wider influence than its actual practice. Its precision and its concentration on form affected artists who did not accept its degree of abstraction, such as Demuth, Sheeler and Schamberg, who for the first time in our history expressed the typically American interest in the machine and its products. Cubism helped our painting to throw off impressionist vagueness, and to return to the clarity that had characterized so much of our earlier art. And in Joseph Stella the United States produced one of the major figures of futurism, whose love of dynamism, speed and spectacularity expressed those traits of the American people.

Abstract art received a strong impetus from the Armory Show, and many pioneer modernists experimented with it. But after a few years most of them (with outstanding exceptions such as O'Keeffe, Dove and Davis) returned to more representational styles. Abstraction had not been, as in Europe, the product of long historical evolution, and most of our artists were not yet ready for so extreme a departure from representation. Not until the middle 1930's did the second wave of abstraction begin to gather force.

By far the most widespread form of modernism in America from the Armory Show to World War II was expressionism. Its wide prevalence can be linked to certain elements in the American mind: our continuing tradition of romanticism; our partiality for art which embodies emotions arising from specific realities; and our preference for free personal expression as against formalism.

All these varieties of modernism were directly related to international modern art. But in the middle 1920's, partly in reaction against international modernism, came a wave of nationalism, a conscious rediscovery of America, still an unexplored continent for most 20th-century American artists. Regionalists such as Benton, Wood and Curry returned to their native Midwest and became articulate champions of the old-fashioned virtues and vices of what they considered the heartland of America. At the same time, Eastern painters such as Hopper, Burchfield, Marsh and Soyer pictured the city and small town with a more drastic realism, a full acceptance of their ugly aspects, but also with a deep emotional attachment. In the work of these portrayers of the American scene, aspects of the United States never touched before were assimilated into art. The American scene painters were a continuation of the interrupted tradition of 19th-century genre, though with little conscious influence, and with greater maturity, realism and emotional depth.

The depression of the 1930's, the rise of fascism, and growing international tensions brought to artists as to everyone else a new realization of the ills of our time. A surge of social protest art swept the country, producing the first full-scale pictorial attack on our social and political system. This school dominated the art world of the mid-1930's; in no other nation did artists say so frankly, loudly and persistently what was wrong with their country—an example of democratic freedom of expression unique in modern history.

Regionalism with its accompanying chauvinism and isolationism could not survive in the modern world; and as for the orthodox social protest school, world events since 1939 rendered its message obsolete. As dominant movements they were replaced by the revived trend to abstraction. But the American scene and social schools together achieved the most far-reaching visual exploration and evaluation of our civilization so far, and made an invaluable contribution to our national self-knowledge. And the best of their work ranks among the most vital achievements of modern American art.

To return to our original question: what qualities of 20th-century American art can be called characteristically American? Obviously, those artists who devoted themselves to the American scene and social order, whether affirmatively or critically, could be products of no other country. But artists speaking in more abstract or semi-abstract language show qualities equally American. To name only a few: John Marin's lyrics of New York and the Maine coast, as pure an expression of our earth and air as the poetry of Walt Whitman or the painting of Winslow Homer; Max Weber's intense expression of the Jewish element in American life; Georgia O'Keeffe's images, abstract or realistic, of the austere beauty of our Southwest; Stuart Davis' powerful designs based on American themes, embodied in form and color as native as jazz. Such widely varied artists, and scores of others, reveal characteristics that are as definitely expressive of our culture as the simpler virtues of our 19th-century artists. Beginning with the realistic rebellion of the 1900's and the advent and absorption of international modernism, American art came of age in the first half of our century, and made increasingly independent and vital contributions to the art of the world.

As to any "American" common denominator, any single quality that might possibly underlie and unify all, I do not believe that, if it exists, it can be isolated and identified by us who are so close to the art of our century. There are many diverse qualities that can be called characteristically American; for ours is a pluralistic art, the expression of a diversified democratic society, giving free rein to wide individualism in artistic creation.

Catalogue

The paintings are presented chronologically. Dimensions are in inches, height before width. The illustrations follow the catalogue, beginning on page 43, and, with the exception of the color plates, are in numerical order.

1   **Three Gravestone Rubbings**
Samuel Walker, Rockingham, Vt. 1798
Rebecca Park and her 14 infants, Grafton,
Vt. 1803
Samuel Taylor, Rockingham, Vt. 1805
By Ann Parker and Avon Neal
Ink on paper
Courtesy Ann Parker and Avon Neal,
North Brookfield, Mass.

Gravestone carvings are the earliest art expression by the English colonists in America. Despite the fact that the carvings are three-dimensional, the designs are conceived in two-dimensional terms. The iconic and highly stylized likenesses first seen on grave markers were eventually translated to canvas.

2   **Mrs. Petrus Vas** (Elsje Rutgers Schuyler
Vas)   *(illus.)*
By the dePeyster limner (working dates
c. 1715–*c.* 1743)
1723. Oil on canvas, 46 × 36½
Courtesy Albany Institute of History and
Art, Albany, N.Y.

This elegant portrait delineated in broad forms and bold outlines is a concept of beauty quite unlike anything that might have been found in Europe at the same time. In recent years—but only on the basis of a third-hand report—it has been ascribed to Pieter Vanderlyn of Kingston, N.Y. It appears more likely that this likeness of the New York-born second wife of Kingston's Domine Petrus Vas is by an artist whose work appears to be confined to New York City and its immediate environs, and whose artistic personality emerges from his portraits of the dePeyster family.

3   **Pau de Wandelaer**   *(illus.)*
Attributed to Pieter Vanderlyn
(1687–1778)
c. 1730. Oil on canvas, 44¾ × 35¼
Courtesy Albany Institute of History and
Art, Albany, N.Y.

This serenely beautiful portrait of a young man, a member of a prosperous Dutch merchant family of Albany, is one of the earliest paintings in which an American landscape is depicted. A typical Hudson River sloop rides at anchor on the river. The boy wears the simple fashions of early 18th-century Albany and the pet goldfinch perched on his outstretched hand is an American bird.

4   **Jacomina Winkler**
By the dePeyster limner
c. 1730. Oil on canvas, 25 × 30
M. Knoedler & Co., N.Y.C.

This portrait of the daughter of a Dutch resident of New York City is a fine example of the work of the early New York artist who depicted members of the dePeyster family. The costume and pose are after Kneller's portrait of Lord Buckhurst and Lady Mary Sackville but the open and clear-eyed face is an unlikely one for members of the English aristocracy.

5   **Lapowinsa**   *(illus.)*
By Gustavus Hesselius (1682–1755)
1735. Oil on canvas, 33 × 25
Courtesy Historical Society of
Pennsylvania, Philadelphia, Pa.

This portrait painted for John, son of William Penn, shows the Delaware Chief Lapowinsa who signed the "Walking Purchase" treaty for lands in Pennsylvania (equitably settled by William Penn but abused by his successors). It conveys the dignity and nobility of a native leader recorded by an American painter born in Sweden.

6   **Abraham Wendell**   *(illus.)*
By the Wendell limner
c. 1737. Oil on ticking, 35⅞ × 29⅝
Courtesy Albany Institute of History and
Art, Albany, N.Y.

This is one of the first American paintings in which an actual scene is depicted. Abraham Wendell's pose and costume follow European convention but the view through the window is of the Wendell's mill on Buttermilk Kill west of Albany. Although most of Albany's population spoke Dutch, several English words appear in the inscriptions on other portraits by the same unidentified artist leading to speculation that he might have come to Albany from England or from another colony.

7   Joseph Sherburne   (illus.)
    By John Singleton Copley (1738–1815)
    c. 1770. Oil on canvas, 50 × 40
    Courtesy Metropolitan Museum of Art
    (Amelia B. Lazarus Fund), N.Y.C.

Until Eakins, Copley was America's greatest portraitist. This painting of Joseph Sherburne shows his genius in highlighting the individuality and character of his subjects. Largely self-taught during his American years, Copley's love of form, texture and light are all visible in this masterful portrayal.

8   Self Portrait at 24   (illus.)
    By Gilbert Stuart (1755–1828)
    1778. Oil on canvas, 16¾ × 12¾
    Courtesy Redwood Library and
    Athenaeum, Newport, R.I.

This portrait, painted early in the period in which Stuart was established in the English studio of Benjamin West, looks back to the artist's American life. Stuart returned to America in 1792, when the subject most in demand here was George Washington. Curiously, this earlier, personal painting impresses one as being a more American statement than his celebrated portraits of the first president.

9   Dr. Philomen Tracy   (illus.)
    By an unidentified painter
    c. 1780. Oil on canvas, 31½ × 29¼
    Courtesy collection of Edgar William
    and Bernice Chrysler Garbisch, N.Y.C.

The direct gaze of the physician conflicts with his grappling for his patient's pulse with his right hand while he grips a vial of medicine in his left. This is, of course, an unusually explicit example of the occupational portraiture of the New Republic. The vitality of the subject is emphasized by a figure that fills the canvas almost beyond its limiting dimensions.

10 Elizabeth Tasker Lowndes   (illus.)
    (Mrs. Christopher Lowndes)
    By Charles Willson Peale (1741–1827)
    1789. Oil on canvas, 20 × 24
    Courtesy of Mr. Tasker G. Lowndes, N.Y.C.

After a period of study in England, Peale returned to this country where he combined his native skill with continental training to translate his subjects' personalities to canvas in direct and forceful terms. This likeness of Elizabeth Lowndes was painted the year of her death, but the bright-eyed subject looks almost like a lively exotic bird with extravagant plumage.

11 Richard Lawson
    Diana James Lawson
    By Charles Peale Polk (1767–1822)
    c. 1794. Oil on canvas, 37½ × 33½ (each)
    M. Knoedler & Co., N.Y.C.

In his youth Polk studied with his uncle, Charles Willson Peale in Philadelphia, and traces of his apprenticeship are visible in these late 18th-century portraits of a Baltimore couple. There is a dry, almost metallic, sharpness in Polk's work that is in contrast to his uncle's sweetness. However, Polk's insistent realism that occasionally moves toward caricature forecasts American painting of the 20th century.

12 Mrs. Ezra Weston, Jr.
    By Rufus Hathaway (1770–1822)
    c. 1795. Oil on canvas
    Courtesy Miss Mary Allis, Fairfield, Conn.

This highly stylized portrait of the daughter-in-law of Duxbury's most prominent citizen is archaic even for the late 18th century. Its direct and forceful terms are reminiscent of the stiff iconic likenesses seen in early 18th-century American gravestone carving.

13 Sarah Prince   (illus.)
    By John Brewster, Jr. (1766–1846)
    c. 1800. Oil on canvas, 50½ × 40
    Courtesy Mr. and Mrs. Jacob M. Kaplan,
    N.Y.C.

There is nothing in Europe to compare with this exact description of a young lady, Sarah Prince of

Newburyport. Sarah Prince was the daughter of a merchant and the artist, John Brewster, Jr., was a deaf mute who traveled back and forth along the New England seacoast following his profession as a portrait painter. By American standards this direct, clear-eyed exchange between artist and subject was—and is—beautiful.

14   **Ephraim Starr**   *(illus.)*
      Hannah Beach Starr
      By Simon Fitch
      1802. Oil on canvas, 58⅝ × 40 1/16 (each)
      Courtesy Wadsworth Atheneum
      (Sumner Collection), Hartford, Conn.

These portraits by Simon Fitch of Lebanon, Conn. are the most monolithic figures in American folk art. The solid bulk of Starr's figure makes it seem to burst from the canvas. Mrs. Starr in her iridescent gown is more placid despite a wandering eye that seems to be an expression of the American realism that became more pronounced as the century progressed.

15   **Pennington Mills, Jones' Falls Valley,**
      Looking Upstream
      By Francis Guy (1760–1820)
      c. 1800. Oil on canvas, 32¾ × 27¼
      Courtesy The Peabody Institute of the City of Baltimore, Baltimore, Md.

Guy started life as a silk dyer, a profession he continued to follow in Brooklyn. On removing to Baltimore in 1798 he took up landscape painting as a full time pursuit; paintings like this one of an American mill were the happy result of the switch in professions.

16   **Clarissa Partridge Childs**
      (Mrs. Asa P. Childs)   *(illus.)*
      Attributed to J. Brown (known working dates: 1807–1812)
      c. 1810. Oil on canvas, 27½ × 23½
      Courtesy Abby Aldrich Rockefeller Folk Art Collection, Williamsburg, Va.

The direct and gentle gaze of the subject in this study in brown and white blends realism with romanticism. Nothing is known of J. Brown beyond his name and a handful of portraits of Massachusetts and southern Vermont subjects but his work evokes a peculiarly American mood.

17   **Harriet Campbell**
      By Ammi Phillips (1788–1865)
      c. 1812. Oil on canvas, 48⅛ × 25
      Courtesy Mr. Oliver F. Eldridge, Canaan, Conn.

This winsome full-length portrait of an American child is one of three girls in similar poses by Ammi Phillips, whose long and prolific history as a portrait painter in inland Massachusetts, Connecticut and New York was observed by John Vanderlyn as "an agreeable way of passing one's time."

Agreeable it may have been as the gentle faces of his women and the handsome ones of men bear testimony, but in a career that lasted sixty years Phillips traveled extensively—within a limited geographical range—altered his style at least five times, and is known today through more than 350 portraits that provide an unparalleled record of the life and times of his contemporaries.

18   **General Schumacker's Daughter** *(a)*
      General Schumacker *(b)*   *(illus.)*
      By Jacob Maentel (1763–1863)
      c. 1812. Pen and watercolor on paper
      a) 14½ × 9½; b) 14⅞ × 10⅛
      Courtesy collection of Edgar William and Bernice Chrysler Garbisch, N.Y.C.

These small scale portraits effectively illustrate the proper concerns of men and women early in the 19th century. Hers is fashion, a house and study (in the German that was the language of many Pennsylvanians until this century); his are battle and the leadership of men.

19   **Captain Samuel Reid**
      By John Wesley Jarvis (1780–1840)
      1815. Oil on canvas, 50½ × 36⅜
      Courtesy Minneapolis Institute of Arts
      (The William Hood Dunwoody Fund), Minneapolis, Minn.

This striking likeness by a New York portraitist of the early 19th century exemplifies the secure, prosperous American, sure of his position in his limited world and society.

20   **Elizabeth Fenimore Cooper**   *(illus.)*
      (Mrs. William Cooper)
      signed: Mr. Freeman
      c. 1816. Watercolor on cardboard,
      17½ × 21¼
      Courtesy New York State Historical Association, Cooperstown, N.Y.

This portrait of the mother of James Fenimore Cooper posed in Otsego Hall, her home in Cooperstown, leaves little doubt about the dominant figure in a classic American family.

21 The Shop and Warehouse of Duncan Phyfe *(illus.)*
By an unidentified artist
c. 1820. Watercolor, 15¾ × 18⅞
Courtesy Metropolitan Museum of Art, N.Y.C.

This precise naive view of three beautiful urban buildings gives unexpected, delightful glimpses into the lives of early 19th-century New Yorkers.

22 Independent Beggar
By Samuel L. Waldo (1736–1861)
c. 1819. Oil on canvas, 32¾ × 25½
Courtesy Boston Athenaeum, Boston, Mass.

This study by Waldo is a striking illustration of the American state of mind that expressed itself in the strident claim that "I'm as good as you are."

23 View from Bluehill, Maine *(illus.)*
By Jonathan Fisher (1768–1847)
c. 1824. Oil on canvas, 26½ × 46½
Courtesy Hirschl & Adler Galleries, N.Y.C.

Bluehill was the home of Jonathan Fisher: minister, linguist, inventor, naturalist, engraver—and painter, whose vision of the Maine coastal landscape is altogether unique and dazzling.

24 The Plantation *(illus.)*
By an unidentified artist
c. 1825. Oil on wood panel, 19¾ × 29½
Courtesy Metropolitan Museum of Art (gift of Edgar William and Bernice Chrysler Garbisch), N.Y.C.

While this fantasy may be based on a real plantation, the arrangement of pond and hill to accommodate trees, grapevine, leafy willow and wild flowers, emerges more as an imaginative and beautiful design than as a reliable record of American estate planning.

25 Scene from "The Last of the Mohicans" *(illus.)*
By Thomas Cole (1801–1848)
1827. Oil on canvas, 25⁵⁄₁₆ × 34¹⁵⁄₁₆
Courtesy Wadsworth Atheneum (bequest of Alfred Smith) Hartford, Conn.

This romantic scene by the young leader of the Hudson River School typifies the 19th-century American artist's rapture with his country and its history. The subject matter reveals the close ties that existed between artists and writers of this period.

26 View of Table Rock and Horseshoe Falls from Below *(illus.)*
By George Catlin (1796–1872)
1827. Oil on canvas, 15¾ × 20½
Courtesy Abby Aldrich Rockefeller Folk Art Collection (gift of Winthrop Rockefeller), Williamsburg, Va.

The power and force of Niagara is frozen in paint in this closeup view of Horseshoe Falls recorded by George Catlin early in his painting career. One of five studies of the Falls by Catlin, the hard-edged line that characterizes his later works appears here in a composition that works as a design as much as it provides a realistic view of a natural wonder.

27 On the Ammonoosuc River
By Henry Cheever Pratt (1803–1880)
c. 1828. Oil on canvas, 25¼ × 30¼
Courtesy Boston Museum of Fine Arts (M. & M. Karolik Collection) Boston, Mass.

From Henry Cheever Pratt's sketchbook: "Tuesday 7th . . . I reluctantly took leave of my interesting travelling companion [Thomas Cole] and started alone on horseback . . . one of the best scenes which I have sketched is . . . in front of a fine rapid in the Ammonoosuc R.—the water falls about 25 ft. in 4 rods over a shelving ledge of granite—in the Centre of the Picture, Mount Washington is in full view—the trees rise on each side just as an artist could wish."

28 The Peaceable Kingdom *(illus.)*
By Edward Hicks (1780–1849)
c. 1830. Oil on canvas, 30 × 35⅞
Courtesy collection of Edgar William and Bernice Chrysler Garbisch, N.Y.C.

This intense and personal expression by the Quaker mystic, preacher, sign- and carriage-painter, Edward Hicks, is one of more than sixty versions by him that still exist. Hicks' own inner torment was immediately exorcised in these paintings in which Penn's Holy Experiment in Pennsylvania is sublimated to the tensions of life as it is—symbolized by the wild and domestic creatures that co-exist on the right.

29   **Leather Stocking Meets the Law**
By John Quidor (1801–1881)
1832. Oil on canvas, 27 × 34
Courtesy New York State Historical
Association, Cooperstown, N.Y.

One of the most surrealistically inclined of American romantic painters, John Quidor's skills were admirably in tune with the literary works of Cooper and Irving that he chose to illustrate. Dreamlike and fragmented, this illustration brings to life a scene from an American classic.

30   **Hunting the Buffalo with Bow and Arrow**
By George Catlin (1796–1872)
c. 1835. Oil on canvas, 32 × 25¾
Courtesy National Cowboy Hall of Fame,
Oklahoma City, Okla.

The years from 1830 to 1839 that Catlin spent in the West were those of his major work as a painter. The lively action paintings of these years of Western expansion were also among the earliest and most poignant American records of wildlife in flight.

31   **Ellen Tuttle Bangs**   *(illus.)*
By Erastus Salisbury Field (1805–1900)
c. 1835. Oil on canvas, 58⅜ × 30¼
Courtesy Metropolitan Museum of Art,
N.Y.C.

The figure is rigid, impersonal and without solidity; still it appears larger than life. It seems to thrust against the outer dimensions of the canvas in an energetic and colorful composition that is characteristic of Erastus Salisbury Field's portraits of his Connecticut Valley friends and relations.

32   **Captain Smith of New London**   *(illus.)*
By Isaac Sheffield (1798–1845)
c. 1835. Oil on wood panel, 33 × 26⅞
Courtesy Museum of American Folk Art
(gift of Mrs. Henry T. Curtiss) N.Y.C.

The whaling captain might be Ahab ashore. The painter, Isaac Sheffield, is known for his portraits of New London whaling families and in this instance has specified Captain Smith's ship, the *Chelsea*, in the background. Strips of blubber are being lifted from a dead whale to the trying out kettles on the vessel's deck.

33   **Lady with Birthmark** *(color, illus. p. 11)*
By Isaac Sheffield (1798–1845)
c. 1835. Oil on canvas, 36 × 22
Courtesy Museum of American Folk Art
(gift of Ann Rockefeller Coste) N.Y.C.

This portrait, found in New London, is almost the size and is framed the same as the portrait of Capt. Smith, also by Isaac Sheffield; it seems likely that this enchanting likeness may be a companion portrait of the sea captain's wife.

34   **William Whipper**   *(illus.)*
By William Matthew Prior (1806–1873)
c. 1835. Oil on canvas, 24¼ × 19⅞
Courtesy New York State Historical
Association, Cooperstown, N.Y.

Working first in Maine and then in the Boston area, Prior advertised his "Painting Garret" to prospective portrait customers. As a member of the Millerites, who believed that the end of the world would occur in 1843, he met many prosperous Negro members and recorded their likenesses with great verve and style as in this painting of William Whipper.

35   **Skating Scene**
By John Toole (1815–1860)
c. 1835. Oil on canvas, 14⅝ × 18⅛
Courtesy National Gallery of Art,
Washington, D.C.

The antics of the ice hockey players are in curious contrast to the placidity of the village and the mountains that surround the scene.

36   **Self Portrait**   *(illus.)*
By Jonathan Fisher (1768–1847)
1838. Oil on canvas, 31 × 27
Courtesy Mr. Robert L. Fisher, Litchfield,
Conn.

This is one of four self portraits done for his children by the Maine parson and painter, Jonathan Fisher. Another of this extraordinary

42. *The Whaler's Flag*, by an unidentified artist

neo-Renaissance gentleman's many talents is exhibited in the Hebrew Bible, one of the languages in which he was fluent. Static and stiff as the portrait is, it bears the imprint of a forceful personality despite its technical limitations. In many respects this direct interpretation shows the pride and independence that were among the traits of American character most remarked upon by visitors to this country.

37 Ohio River Landscape (illus.)
By an unidentified artist
c. 1820. Oil on canvas, 19½ × 28
Courtesy Mr. and Mrs. Samuel Schwartz, Paterson, N.J.

This peaceful view of country life along the Ohio by an unidentified painter shows a prosperous self-contained world in which two early side-wheelers and an extraordinary plantation and mill of the early 19th century are highlighted.

38 Diagram of Contrasts (illus.)
By Thomas Cole (1801–1848)
c. 1834. Oil on a wood panel, 25 × 35
Courtesy Mrs. Barbara E. Johnson, Princeton, N.J.

This diagram of contrasts illustrates Cole's interest in a rational theory of color. The gradation of color within each segment of the wheel recalls Cezanne's experiments in implying form and changing planes by contrasts of light and dark.

39 Political Banner (illus.)
By Terence Kennedy (c. 1820–?)
1844. Oil on fabric, 73 in. diameter
Courtesy New York State Historical Association, Cooperstown, N.Y.

The New York State countryside of the 1840s is reflected in this large round canvas by Terence J. Kennedy of Auburn. The painting records the country's progress: riches of field, stream and industry are guarded by an oversized eagle—as the Erie Canal finds its way through the Hudson River channel to the open sea.

40 Rebecca Alston Hayne
(Mrs. Robert Y. Hayne)
By Samuel F. B. Morse (1791–1872)
c. 1845. Oil on canvas, 30 × 25
M. Knoedler & Co., N.Y.C.

Morse treats the subject in almost modern terms; the attractive portrait is typical of many by the artist-inventor who had great influence as an art teacher and as one of the founders and first president of the National Academy of Design.

41 Fair of the American Institute at Niblo's Garden
By Benjamin Harrison
c. 1845. Gouache, 20¼ × 27½
Courtesy Museum of the City of New York, N.Y.C.

After the amazing fair-in-the-city opened in 1845, Benjamin Harrison, a tanner and chairmaker by profession, rapidly sketched its catalog of eclectic wonders that ranged from paintings by Erastus Field to a collection of one hundred pieced quilts and a case of spectacles. The resulting painting, a late entry in the revised catalog of the fair, shows the miscellany against the vaulted interior of the exhibition hall of Niblo's Garden.

42 The Whaler's Flag (color, illus. p. 28)
By an unknown artist
c. 1845. Oil on canvas, 39 × 95½
Courtesy Mr. Dan W. Lufkin, N.Y.C.

Recently discovered in New London, Connecticut, this huge canvas is an early instance of the heroic pictorial display of the national standard. It is also a rare example of the flag being so purposefully related to a distinctive American commercial enterprise.

43 Cat in Open Window (illus.)
By an unidentified artist
c. 1845. Oil on canvas, 22½ × 31¼
Courtesy Mr. and Mrs. Bertram K. Little, Brookline, Mass.

The exercise of fooling the eye into seeing three dimensions in two has always delighted painters. This simple *trompe l'oeil* by an unidentified American painter is one of the most charming of these deceptions.

44 West Hartford Couple (illus.)
Probably by Erastus S. Field (1805–1900)
c. 1845. Oil on canvas, 59½ × 76
Courtesy Mr. and Mrs. J. William Middendorf II, N.Y.C.

Occupying all the space that this large canvas affords, the large-scale figures emphasize the importance of the individual in his society in mid nineteenth-century America. Hartford was one of the locations regularly visited by Erastus Field; there he stayed with his relatives and often painted portraits of them and their friends, an ever present clientele.

45   **The Residence of David Twining in 1785** *(illus.)*
By Edward Hicks (1780–1849)
c. 1845. Oil on canvas, 26¼ × 29⅞
Courtesy Carnegie Institute Museum of Art, Pittsburgh, Pa.

There still exist today four views of Hicks' childhood home at the farm of David Twining in Bucks County. This remembered vision of harmonious neatness shows the farm as it was when the artist was five years old; it brings together vignettes from the real farm and those borrowed from prints and woodcuts. There is an even and staccato beat to this composition in which every figure, building, creature and tree are presented in the same light and with equal emphasis.

46   **Cornell Farm** *(color, illus. p. 34)*
By Edward Hicks (1780–1849)
1848. Oil on canvas, 36¾ × 49
Courtesy National Gallery of Art (gift of Edgar William and Bernice Chrysler Garbisch), Washington, D.C.

Painted the year before his death, this is the next to last Bucks' County scene known by Edward Hicks. Despite the realistic approach to the Cornells and their prize stock, this Indian summer view is almost like a dream remembered. The lines of horses and cattle might have been—in Hicks' mind—an orderly procession to lead him toward an ideal Quaker heaven.

47   **Kindred Spirits** *(color, illus. p. 43)*
By Asher B. Durand (1796–1886)
1849. Oil on canvas, 44 × 36
Courtesy New York Public Library, N.Y.C.

This painting by one of the leading exponents of the Hudson River School shows the kindred spirits, William Cullen Bryant and Durand's fellow artist, Thomas Cole, as they contemplate the American landscape that artists and poets celebrated in the awakened romantic mood of the first half of the 19th century.

48   **Mourning for the Dead**
By Seth Eastman (1808–1875)
1849. Water color on paper, 8 × 6
Courtesy James Jerome Hill Reference Library, St. Paul, Minn.

This small and immediate view into Indian life is one of the paintings done in Texas by an American artist who is best known for his record of Western tribal life.

49   **Sunnyside** *(illus.)*
By George Inness (1825–1894)
c. 1850. Oil on canvas, 14¾ × 19¾
Courtesy Sleepy Hollow Restorations, Tarrytown, N.Y.

In this small, early painting, Innes celebrates the romantic view of nature and provides a portrait of the unique Dutch charm of Sunnyside, Washington Irving's house overlooking the Hudson, where he lived from 1832 until his death in 1859.

50   **Pavilion Beach, Gloucester** *(illus.)*
By Fitz Hugh Lane (1804–1865)
c. 1855. Oil on canvas, 15¼ × 20½
Courtesy Mr. and Mrs. Bertram K. Little, Brookline, Mass.

Lane's layering of space by objects and light is demonstrated in this portrait of Pavilion Point in Gloucester, his home town. The abandoned boat and stone wall establish the foreground, the sailboat the middle ground and the pavilion and town the far distance.

51   **Black Cat on a Chair** *(illus.)*
By Dr. Andrew L. von Wittkamp
c. 1855. Oil on canvas, 36 × 29¼
Courtesy Boston Museum of Fine Arts, Boston, Mass.

The artist's life and work are known only through the evidence presented in this painting. The realistic portrait of a black cat is signed by von Wittkamp with "M.D." following his signature; a label on the stretcher bears the name of a Philadelphia dealer in artist's materials which, along with the room interior, suggests a Pennsylvania provenance.

**52 Reminiscences of the Catskill
Mountains** (*illus.*)
By John Frederick Kensett (1816–1872)
c. 1855. Oil on canvas, 22½ × 18¼
Courtesy Hirschl & Adler Galleries, N.Y.C.

The public recognition that came to Kensett strikes an oddly contemporary chord: he was appointed by President Buchanan to serve on the first Art Commission for the National Capitol and was one of the first trustees of the Metropolitan Museum. The landscape by which he is represented shows his sensitivity to light and his ability to express vast space in the narrow confines of a small canvas.

53 New York State Village
By Joseph H. Hidley (1830–1872)
c. 1855. Oil on canvas, 37 × 53
Courtesy Hirschl & Adler Galleries, N.Y.C.

This view of an unidentified village is probably a New York State scene close to Hidley's home in Poestenkill where he worked not only as a painter but also as a taxidermist and wood carver. Like most of Hidley's landscapes, this is a detailed portrait of one small American village in microcosm.

54 Turkey Shoot (*illus.*)
By Tompkins H. Matteson (1813–1884)
1857. Oil on canvas, 36 × 42
Courtesy New York State Historical
Association, Cooperstown, N.Y.

Matteson's career as an artist closely follows that of John Quidor's; both were inspired by the heroes and plots of romantic American fiction. Although Matteson's best known painting is "The Spirit of '76," this scene is from James Fenimore Cooper's *The Pioneers*. Except for the lively figure of Leather Stocking on the right it is a static illustration like a staging of wax work figures.

55 Shooting Flamingos on the Grand Saline
By George Catlin (1796–1872)
1857. Oil on canvas, 18½ × 26
Courtesy Graham Galleries, N.Y.C.

Almost like a landscape on the moon is this scene of nesting flamingos pink-dotting the landscape. The hunter at lower left is the only intrusion on Catlin's vision.

56 View of Barnstable
By an unidentified artist
c. 1857. Oil on canvas, 36½ × 48½
Courtesy Addison Gallery of American Art,
Andover, Mass.

This delightful view by an unknown artist is a composition of many images that recall the figures and events of a small New England town.

57 War News from Mexico (*illus.*)
By Richard Caton Woodville (1825–1856)
c. 1846. Oil on canvas, 27 × 24¾
Courtesy National Academy of Design,
N.Y.C.

Looking for all the world like a wagon setting for a miracle play is this dramatic scene crowded within the architectural framework of the front porch of an American hotel. Among the painters represented in this show, Woodville was unique in that most of his artistic life was spent abroad in Dusseldorf, London and Paris. He regularly sent his paintings to be exhibited in America, however, and with his selective remembrances of his native country became one of the most popular of its genre painters.

58 View of Sacramento California (*illus.*)
By George Tirrell
c. 1860. Oil on canvas, 27 × 47¾
Courtesy Museum of Fine Arts
(Karolik Collection), Boston, Mass.

This view of a bustling west coast city and its riverfront at mid-century is probably copied from a print which may explain the lively 20th-century beat given to a 19th-century theme.

59 Corn Husking (*illus.*)
By Eastman Johnson (1824–1906)
1860. Oil on canvas, 26 × 30
Courtesy Everson Museum of Art,
Syracuse, N.Y.

As the son of Maine's Secretary of State, Johnson grew up in a political atmosphere. However, it was his own real skill as a portrait painter that brought him his famous clients. This talent for portraying character was also set to use in genre paintings like this one—highly realistic, selectively detailed and highlighted and shadowed to bring three separate scenes together into one carefully organized composition.

60 Bare Knuckles *(illus.)*
By George A. Hayes (1854–1934)
c. 1860. Oil on cardboard, 11 ⅞ × 19 ⅛
Courtesy collection of Edgar William and
Bernice Chrysler Garbisch, N.Y.C.

The manly art of self-defense has long been a
popular subject with American artists. In the mid-
nineteenth century, fist-fighting was a team
sport, and in this painting Hayes depicts two
three-man teams battling it out in the open air in
one of the many contests in defiance of U.S. law.
The last bare knuckles fight in America, the
Sullivan-Kilrain bout of 1889, went seventy-five
rounds.

61 Wildflowers in a Glass Vase *(illus.)*
By an unidentified artist
c. 1860. Oil on canvas, 16 ¾ × 19 ⅝
Courtesy Mr. and Mrs. George A. Stern,
N.Y.C.

The pleasure in simple things is the focus on
which this unknown painter set his eye. The composition is a disunited one but emphasizes the
untutored artist's pleasure in canvases that are
filled with detail.

62 Mother and Son *(illus.)*
By William A. Walker (1838–1921)
c. 1860. Oil on canvas, 12 × 9
Courtesy Estate of Joseph B. Martinson,
N.Y.C.

This painting illustrates a Southern variation on
an ancient theme at the time of the Civil War.

**63 After the Wedding in Warren,
Pennsylvania** *(illus.)*
By an unidentified artist
c. 1862. Oil on canvas, 22 ½ × 30 ¼
Courtesy collection of Edgar William and
Bernice Chrysler Garbisch, N.Y.C.

An oil boom brought prosperity to Warren in the
1860s. The house on the hill is Cobham's Castle
(in honor of its owner, an Englishman) and the
factory on the right later became the home of
Piso's Cure for Consumption. The domed building
in the foreground is the courthouse. The town's
life, its weddings and the regular arrivals of train
and steamboat are all captured in this permanent
record of a festive moment in time.

**64 General Doubleday Watching His
Troops Cross the Potomac** *(illus.)*
Attributed to David Blythe (1815–1865)
c. 1863. Oil on canvas, 29 ½ × 40
Courtesy National Baseball Hall of Fame
and Museum, Inc., Cooperstown, N.Y.

In a remarkably pastoral setting, Union troops
are depicted in orderly pursuit of Lee's Army of
Northern Virginia—which in June 1863 was moving north to Pennsylvania after its victory at
Chancellorsville.

65 Stag at Echo Rock *(illus.)*
By an unidentified artist
c. 1865. Oil on canvas, 36 × 29
Courtesy Mr. Herbert W. Hemphill, Jr.,
N.Y.C.

This view of a stag in winter is a fantasy approach
to a real scene—Echo Rock at Mountain View,
N.J. The jagged rocks, bare tree branches and
stag's antlers make a fascinating and repetitive
design that divides the canvas into patterns like a
medieval tapestry. The stag itself recalls the
popular insurance figure that Yankee enterprise
fixed on the national consciousness.

66 Garden of Eden
By Erastus Salisbury Field (1805–1900)
c. 1865. Oil on canvas, 35 × 41 ½
Courtesy Shelburne Museum, Shelburne,
Vermont

While Field borrowed his composition for this
painting from Thomas Cole's illustrations for the
Divine Comedy, the end result is as much based on
Field's own Connecticut Valley landscape as any
other. It is typical of folk art that the Garden of
Eden should depend as much on what the artist
knows about the land around him as on what he
has learned.

67 Third Avenue Railroad Depot
By H. Schenck
c. 1860. Oil on canvas, 36 ¼ × 50 ¼
Courtesy Metropolitan Museum of Art
(bequest of Edward W. C. Arnold), N.Y.C.

This precise record of New York's Third Avenue
Railroad was painted for the president of the line,
William A. Darling. A balloon ascension, the
weather vane in the form of a horse-drawn trolley,
the company of N.Y. Volunteers, and the individ-
ualized spectators make this a valuable commen-
tary on New York life at midcentury.

46. *Cornell Farm*, by Edward Hicks

68 General Francis B. Spinola
By William Sydney Mount (1807–1868)
1867. Oil on canvas, 34 × 27
Courtesy Graham Galleries, N.Y.C.

Although Mount's reputation is based chiefly on his genre paintings, this portrait, painted the year before his death, is typical of the many on which he depended for his principal support throughout his lifetime.

69 Mount Whitney *(illus.)*
By Albert Bierstadt (1830–1902)
1869. Oil on canvas, 36 × 54
Courtesy Newark Museum, Newark, N.J.

Bierstadt's characteristically luminous terrain, touched with a changing play of light and shadow, appears in this awesome view. The painter's sojourns in Dusseldorf and Rome are revealed in his mastery of technique but his immediate inspiration is the American West.

70 Salt Hay on the Rowley *(illus.)*
By Martin Johnson Heade (1819–1904)
c. 1870. Oil on canvas, 13¼ × 26¼
Courtesy Hirschl & Adler Galleries, N.Y.C.

The incredible and mystical light on the salt marsh is like a scene on another planet. This highly personal and romantic view of nature—as it is intensified in the painter's mind and purified once more as his brush records it—bears comparison with some of the equally personal but far less empty landscapes painted by Heade's earliest teacher, Edward Hicks.

71 The Christmas Bell
By John Ferguson Weir (1841–1926)
c. 1870. Oil on canvas, 33⅛ × 20⅛
Courtesy Century Club, N.Y.C.

This illustration of Poe's poem was painted by a nephew of the more celebrated J. Alden Weir long after its subject had become a fixed feature in the American imagination.

72 Barnegat Bay *(illus.)*
By Francis Silva (1835–1886)
c. 1870. Oil on canvas, 11⅞ × 19⅞
Courtesy Hirschl & Adler Galleries, N.Y.C.

A light-struck landscape related to those of Martin Heade and Fitz Hugh Lane is now inhabited with houses and people. While part of the enchantment disappears, an association with remembered experience remains.

73 View of Benjamin Reber's Farm *(illus.)*
By Charles C. Hofmann
(working dates: mid-19th century)
1872. Oil on canvas, 25¼ × 34⅞
Courtesy National Gallery of Art
(gift of Edgar William and Bernice Chrysler Garbisch), Washington, D.C.

This precise vision of a Bucks County farm forecasts John Kane's views of Pittsburgh in its orderly division of space. Hofmann, like three other voluntary inmates of nineteenth-century Pennsylvania poor houses, worked to record his own immediate surroundings and the appearance of life on nearby farms.

74 John Biglen in a Single Scull *(illus.)*
By Thomas Eakins (1844–1916)
c. 1874. Water color on paper, 17⅛ × 23
Courtesy Metropolitan Museum of Art
(Fletcher Fund), N.Y.C.

This water color is one of several variations by Eakins on the same theme. The solitary figure sculling on a sunlit river shows Eakins' new and unique way of looking at figures and objects in sunlight.

75 The New Novel *(illus.)*
By Winslow Homer (1836–1910)
c. 1877. Water color on paper, 9½ × 20½
Courtesy Museum of Fine Arts, Springfield, Mass.

This small, evocative work by Homer illustrates his lyrical romanticizing of commonplace incidents.

76 Ballance Dry Dock *(illus.)*
By Frederick Huge
c. 1877. Tempera, 23½ × 35
Courtesy Mr. and Mrs. Jacob M. Kaplan, N.Y.C.

In this small painting the artist has recorded a wealth of information on New York City life.

77 Martha J. Lamb
By Cornelia Adele Fassett
c. 1878. Oil on canvas, 15 × 24
Courtesy New-York Historical Society,
N.Y.C.

This painting is the quintessence of upper class
American life late in the 19th century. It could
be an illustration for an Edith Wharton novel; in
fact, it is a portrait of an energetic New York lady
who, among other achievements, was the first
woman to address a meeting of the New-York
Historical Society.

78 Old West Parlor *(a)*   *(illus.)*
East Chamber *(b)*
East Parlor *(c)*
By Ella Emery
c. 1878. Oil on canvas
a) 13¾ × 17½; *b)* 15½ × 26¾;
c) 15½ × 21½
Courtesy Mr. and Mrs. Bertram K. Little,
Brookline, Mass.

This is an exact pictorial catalog of the possessions
and decoration in the Peter Cushing House in
Hingham, Mass. in the Victorian era. The house
is still owned by descendants. Some of the furnish-
ings seen here—and conveying the provincial
New England mood of the decade that followed
the Civil War—remain in the house today.

79 Harvest Moon   *(color, illus. p. 65)*
By George Inness (1825–1894)
1886. Oil on canvas, 39 × 29½
Courtesy Graham Galleries, N.Y.C.

This study of an autumnal scene in night light,
a late work by one of the best of America's 19th-
century landscape painters, illustrates his special
ability to set mood and scene within two dimensions.

80 The Newsboy   *(illus.)*
By George Newell Bowers
c. 1889. Oil on canvas, 18 × 14½
Courtesy Museum of Fine Arts, Springfield,
Mass.

A precise moment in the well organized daily life
of a prosperous western Massachusetts city of the
late 19th century is captured here in a composition
which is derived from the Dutch genre painters
of the 17th century. The artist's studio in the

Court Square Building in Springfield is described
down to the mat at the door and the mechanism
to open the transom. (The heart of the building,
once the Court Square Theatre, has been demol-
ished and is now a parking lot.)

81 The Morning Bell   *(illus.)*
By Winslow Homer (1836–1910)
Oil on canvas, 24 × 38¼
Courtesy Yale University Art Gallery
(bequest of Stephen C. Clark), New Haven,
Conn.

Homer's special genius for turning commonplace
American experience into an evocative symbolic
image is seldom displayed better than in this view
of a teacher—alone—on her way up a narrow
land bridge to a building more reminiscent of the
Ark than a country school.

82 The Clock   *(illus.)*
By John Haberle (1858–1933)
c. 1890. Oil on canvas, 26 × 15½
Courtesy Hirschl & Adler Galleries, N.Y.C.

One of Haberle's most delightful tricks of decep-
tion is this mantel clock painted on a canvas
stretched over a box frame. The cracked glass in
the reverse-painted scene below and the twisted
string that replaces the knob are devices that lend
reality to the painted vision.

83 The Old Birch
By Homer Martin (1836–1897)
c. 1890. Oil on canvas, 24 × 15¼
Courtesy Paine Art Center, Oshkosh, Wis.

Born in Albany when the Hudson River School
was at the height of its creativity and influence,
Martin was in his mid-fifties before he settled on
a career as an artist. His instruction in art came
through extended visits to England and France
but the appearance of the American landscape
was a more obvious influence.

84 Hound and Hunter   *(color, illus. p. 17)*
By Winslow Homer (1836–1910)
c. 1892. Water color, 12½ × 19½
Courtesy M. Knoedler & Co., N.Y.C.

Painting's two dimensions often seem to present
a glimpse of life through a small window. Rarely
is the quality more evident than in this captured

moment of a hunter gliding with his prey through an enchanted swamp and forest.

85   Trumpeter Swan   *(illus.)*
      By Alexander Pope (1849–1924)
      c. 1900. Oil on canvas, 57 × 44½
      Courtesy Mr. and Mrs. J. William
      Middendorf II, N.Y.C.

Alexander Pope was primarily a portraitist whose subjects were mostly members of Boston society. In this painting of an all but extinct bird he transcends his customary vivid realism and creates a recognizable symbol of the crucifixion.

86   Sportsman's Trophy   *(illus.)*
      By Alexander Pope (1849–1924)
      1898–1899. Oil on canvas, 48 × 51½
      M. Knoedler & Co., N.Y.C.

The organization of this large and ebullient *trompe l'oeil* painting is interesting for its similarity to Pope's *Trumpeter Swan* (also in this exhibition). Once again, the arrangement provides a secondary image; here the knapsack and dead grouse recreate the mask of the moose whose rack of horns supports the hunter's guns, his shot, powder and whisky.

87   The Thinker   *(illus.)*
      By Thomas Eakins (1844–1916)
      1900. Oil on canvas, 82 × 42
      Courtesy Metropolitan Museum of Art
      (Kennedy Fund), N.Y.C.

This extraordinary full-length portrait is a classic display of Eakins' genius for highlighting individuality and character through close observation and transcription of the mass and form of the human figure.

88   Fifth Avenue and 34th Street
      By Everett Shinn (1876–1953)
      1905. Oil on canvas, 20 × 30
      M. Knoedler & Co. Inc., N.Y.C.

While New York was endlessly photographed from the moment the camera was developed, it was the early 20th-century painters who suggested best the energy and vigor of the life they knew here. In this painting it is not the architecture of the bustling city that dominates the scene but the people who move along its streets. (The shop in the foreground was the site of Knoedler's from 1878 to 1911.)

89   Club Night at Sharkey's   *(illus.)*
      By George Bellows (1882–1925)
      c. 1907. Oil on canvas, 40 × 50
      Courtesy Mr. John Hay Whitney, N.Y.C.

One of Bellows' geniuses is in capturing motion and turbulence so exactly that the viewer completes the action in his mind's eye.

90   Gold Panners' Camp—Big Horn
      Mountains, 1909   *(color, illus. p. 68)*
      By Frederic Remington (1861–1909)
      c. 1909. Oil on canvas, 27 × 30
      Courtesy National Cowboy Hall of Fame,
      Oklahoma City, Okla.

Painted in the last year of his life, this mining camp scene by Remington has an other-worldly quality. One of his night scenes, it is a close-up view that is mystically colored but strangely impersonal.

91   Cinch Ring   *(illus.)*
      By Charles M. Russell (1864–1926)
      c. 1909. Oil on canvas, 24 × 36½
      Courtesy National Cowboy Hall of Fame,
      Oklahoma City, Okla.

Painted on commission for reproduction as a color print, this anecdotal work exemplifies Russell's popular image of the American cowboy.

92   The White Horse
      By George Bellows (1882–1925)
      Oil on canvas, 34⅛ × 44⅟₁₆
      Courtesy Worcester Art Museum,
      Worcester, Mass.

At first the white horse of the title seems incidental, yet it leads the viewer into the scene almost like a unicorn in medieval legend.

93   Sunday, Women Drying Their Hair
      By John Sloan (1871–1951)
      c. 1912. Oil on canvas, 25½ × 31½
      Courtesy Addison Gallery of American Art,
      Andover, Mass.

The play of bright sun on the human figure dramatizes a homely incident in New York City life in the early part of the century. The attention paid to masses of hair as an adornment recalls the central action of O. Henry's *Gift of the Magi*.

94 Merry-Go-Round
By Maurice Prendergast (1859–1924)
c. 1912. Oil on canvas, 14¼ × 19¼
M. Knoedler & Co., N.Y.C.

The use of light and color in this painting is impressionistic, yet the subject is a typically American one, showing how a basically European art form could be successfully adapted to the native scene.

95 Backyards, Greenwich Village *(illus.)*
By John Sloan (1871–1951)
c. 1914. Oil on canvas, 26 × 32
Courtesy Whitney Museum of American Art, N.Y.C.

The fleeting moment became the special province of American realist painters of the early 20th century. Painted on the eve of the first World War, this mundane scene of a sudden deep snow fall in the city mysteriously combines the essence of its own time with a spirit of timelessness.

96 Pine Tree
By John Marin (1870–1953)
1914. Water color on paper, 19¼ × 16⅞
Courtesy Vassar College Art Gallery (gift of Paul Rosenfeld), Poughkeepsie, N.Y.

Marin's variations on nature, his skill in suggesting abstract designs from real things and his joyous use of the water color medium result in works that crackle with energy.

97 Indian Composition
By Marsden Hartley (1877–1943)
c. 1915. Oil on canvas, 47 × 47
Courtesy Vassar College Art Gallery (gift of Paul Rosenfeld), Poughkeepsie, N.Y.

Composed like an Indian sand painting, this work registers first as an abstraction, but woven in and out of its structure are Indian symbols, totems and designs.

98 Manchester Valley *(illus.)*
By Joseph Pickett
c. 1915. Oil with sand on canvas, 45½ × 60⅝
Courtesy Museum of Modern Art (gift of Abby Aldrich Rockefeller), N.Y.C.

Like other folk painters before him, the 20th-century painter Joseph Pickett felt compelled to portray his awareness of every branch and leaf. Despite his concern for detail the composition has an even and regular beat. Perspective is abandoned; the form is what the artist knows exists and not what his eye really sees.

99 Allies Day
By Childe Hassam (1859–1935)
1917. Oil on canvas, 36¾ × 30¼
Courtesy National Gallery of Art, Washington, D.C.

The fragility of the flags moving in the breeze contrasts with the stability of buildings gleaming in the sun; both dominate the crowds of antlike people that swarm through the city's streets in a scene that captures the moment and mood of World War I.

100 The Sale of Marblehead to the Indians for Eighty Dollars (1684) *(illus.)*
By J. O. J. Frost
c. 1919. Oil on academy board, 15½ × 36¼
Courtesy Mr. and Mrs. George A. Stern, N.Y.C.

The 20th-century folk artist J. O. J. Frost painted numerous reminiscences of events in the history of Marblehead, his home town. Each segment of this highly patterned painting illustrates a different town legend.

101 Landscape Fantasy
By Marsden Hartley (1877–1943)
c. 1922. Oil on canvas, 27½ × 21¼
Courtesy New York University Art Collection, N.Y.C.

The changing landscape becomes a curving abstraction in the powerful form and moving line with which Hartley charges this composition.

102 Bucks County Barn *(illus.)*
By Charles Sheeler (1883–1965)
1923. Tempera and crayon, 19¼ × 25¼
Courtesy Whitney Museum of American Art, N.Y.C.

The elimination of extraneous detail and the immaculate and exact delineation of form are characteristic of this artist who speaks for an age of technology but whose vocabulary seems to be drawn from Shaker furniture and functional rural architecture.

103 American Synchromy No. 1 (Green)
By Stanton MacDonald-Wright (1890–   )
c. 1925. Oil on canvas, 23 × 34½
M. Knoedler & Co., N.Y.C.

One of the American painters to formulate the
color theories of synchromism in Paris in 1913,
Wright returned to this country soon after. While
the synchromist group continued to apply their
theories to abstraction, Wright extended his study
of color organization and harmony to the human
figure.

104 The Bootleggers
                    (color, illus. frontispiece)
By Thomas Hart Benton (1889–1969)
c. 1927. Oil on canvas, 72 × 65
M. Knoedler & Co., N.Y.C.

Benton credits his work with the Navy as an
architectural draftsman as "... the most impor-
tant event in my development as an artist ...
I was forced to observe the objective character
of ... buildings, airplanes, dredges, and ships—
things so interesting in themselves that I forgot
my aesthetic drivellings and morbid self-concerns.
I left once for all my little world of art for art's
sake and entered into a world which ... I had not
seen. That was the world of America."

105 Hill in Pittsburgh
By John Kane (1860–1934)
1928. Oil on canvas, 18½ × 22½
M. Knoedler & Co., N.Y.C.

The self-taught artist's special instinct to divide
and order his canvas is especially evident in the
work of the 20-century folk painter John Kane.
The design and composition of this real hill in
Pittsburgh invites comparison with abstractions
that Kane's more worldly contemporaries were
beginning to create in the late 1920s.

106 Self Portrait   *(illus.)*
By John Kane (1860–1934)
1929. Oil on canvas over composition
board, 36⅛ × 27⅛
Courtesy Museum of Modern Art
(Abby Aldrich Rockefeller Fund), N.Y.C.

Archaic and stylized as an early New England
portrait, this symmetrical self study by a modern
painter has equal power and intensity.

107 Woman with Plants   *(illus.)*
By Grant Wood (1892–1942)
c. 1929. Oil on panel board, 20½ × 17½
Courtesy Cedar Rapids Fine Arts
Association, Cedar Rapids, Iowa

Wood's ability to create powerful and evocative
compositions from simple incidents and materials
made him one of America's most popular artists
of the 1930s and 1940s.

108 Buildings, Lancaster
By Charles Demuth (1883–1935)
c. 1930. Oil on composition board, 24 × 20
Courtesy Whitney Museum of American
Art, N.Y.C.

The 19th-century buildings of a long established
firm are depicted in a contrived 20th-century
cubist style.

109 John Brown Going to his Hanging
By Horace Pippin (1898–1946)
c. 1942. Oil on canvas, 24 × 30
Courtesy Pennsylvania Academy
of Fine Arts, Philadelphia, Pa.

This recollection of John Brown by a 20th-century
Negro artist is powerful in its simplicity. Dark
earth tones contrasting with large areas of white
paint heighten the mourning mood.

110 Mrs. Gamley   *(illus.)*
By George Luks (1867–1933)
c. 1930. Oil on canvas, 66 × 48
Courtesy Whitney Museum of American
Art, N.Y.C.

This monolithic figure of an old woman in an
old-fashioned kitchen with its pump and iron
stove is outlined in spare and economical terms,
but the power that lies in this nearly life-size
painting extends forward from the canvas as from
an actor on a stage.

111 Carlock
By Walter Murch (1907–1967)
c. 1937. Oil on panel, 26¾ × 18¾
Courtesy Mr. Anthony Bower, N.Y.C.

The fluidity and perfection of the machine become
the subject for painters like Murch who emphasize
and select its special characteristics as in this
portrayal of a car lock.

**112 The Passion of Sacco
and Vanzetti** *(illus.)*
By Ben Shahn (1898–1969)
c. 1931–32. Tempera on canvas, 84½ × 48
Courtesy Whitney Museum of American
Art, N.Y.C.

"At some point very early in my life I became
absorbed—not in man's fate, but rather in man's
state. The question of suffering is an eternal
mystery. . . . but its reality impinges upon us
everywhere. . . . Whatever my basic promptings
and urges may be, I am aware that the concern,
the compassion for suffering—feeling it, formu-
lating it—has been the constant intention of my
work since I first picked up a paint brush."
Ben Shahn, 1961.

113 Evening
By Charles Burchfield (1893–   )
1932. Watercolor on paper, 31½ × 43½
Courtesy Newark Museum, Newark, N.J.

In this view Burchfield turns the edge of life from
hopelessness into a romantic—almost a senti-
mental—scene in which the resurgence of spring
is contrasted with the twilight hour.

114 The Buffalo Hunt *(illus.)*
By Horace Pippin (1898–1946)
1933. Oil on canvas, 21¼ × 31
Courtesy Whitney Museum of American
Art, N.Y.C.

The stark, bold patterns of this work give a forceful impression of lonely and untamed land.

115 Landscape near Chicago
By Aaron Bohrod (1907–   )
1934. Oil on composition board, 24 × 32
Courtesy Whitney Museum of American
Art, N.Y.C.

Rarely has the affinity that exists between 19th-
century folk artists and the painters of the 1930s
been so exactly affirmed as in this painting by
Aaron Bohrod.

116 Coal Barge
By Aaron Bohrod (1907–   )
c. 1935. Oil on canvas, 15½ × 14
Courtesy New York University
Art Collection, N.Y.C.

This view of a Great Lake coal barge at dock sets
a dark mood of social protest.

117 Early Sunday Morning *(illus.)*
By Edward Hopper (1882–1967)
c. 1935. Oil on canvas, 35 × 60
Courtesy Whitney Museum of American
Art, N.Y.C.

The loneliness and isolation of those adrift in
American urban life are Hopper's reiterated
themes stated even in ghost-haunted city landscapes like this one, actually empty of people.

118 O, Chautauqua *(illus.)*
By Grant Wood (1892–1942)
c. 1935. Pencil and colored crayon on paper,
15½ × 14¼
Courtesy M. Knoedler & Co., N.Y.C.

Drawn as the jacket illustration for Thomas Duncan's book, *O Chautauqua*, Grant Wood's composition resembles a great spider web. His elevated
point of view reduces known objects to an abstract
design.

119 American Farm
By Joe Jones (1909–   )
1936. Oil and tempera on canvas, 30 × 40
Courtesy Whitney Museum of American
Art, N.Y.C.

This tortured view of an eroded farm in the dust
bowl might be an illustration for Steinbeck's
Grapes of Wrath.

120 Acrobat in Maroon and Blue
By Walt Kuhn (1880–1949)
1938. Oil on canvas, 24 × 20
M. Knoedler & Co., N.Y.C.

Kuhn's skill in showing more than surface appearance is illustrated in this portrait in which
the tinselled costume heightens the subject's
introverted and haunted face.

121 Hopscotch
By Loren MacIver (1909–   )
1940. Oil on canvas, 27 × 35⅞
Courtesy Museum of Modern Art, N.Y.C.

Loren MacIver's special ability to anchor the
abstract to reality is demonstrated in this painting
which may be viewed in either light.

122 Fisherman's Last Supper *(illus.)*
By Marsden Hartley (1877–1943)
1940–41. Oil on canvas, 30 × 41
Courtesy Mr. and Mrs. Roy R. Neuberger,
N.Y.C.

The content of Hartley's memorial *agape* is grief and mourning; in form it is as stark and bold as an archaic sculpture.

123 Girl in Stars and Bars   *(illus.)*
By Morris Hirschfield (1872–1946)
c. 1943. Oil on canvas, 45½ × 35½
Courtesy Mr. Edward A. Bragaline, N.Y.C.

Morris Hirschfield, the cloak and suit manufacturer turned painter, exhibits his fascination with texture and design in this painting on a 20th-century American theme constructed like a medieval banner.

124 Seated Girl with Dog   *(illus.)*
By Milton Avery (1893–)
c. 1944. Oil on canvas, 44 × 32
Courtesy Mr. and Mrs. Roy Neuberger, N.Y.C.

Reduced to simplest terms, reality and individuality become a study in design and color.

125 Jimmy Savo and Rope   *(illus.)*
By Adolf Dehn (1895–1968)
c. 1944. Gouache, 14⅜ × 21⅜
Courtesy Whitney Museum of American Art, N.Y.C.

The comedy and pathos of the little man—even the suggestion that these qualities are akin and have their own isolation and loneliness—are expressed in this small composition in which economy of line and mass are syncopated against the energy of the main figure.

126 Poppy   *(illus.)*
By Georgia O'Keeffe (1887–)
c. 1927. Oil on canvas, 30 × 36
M. Knoedler & Co., N.Y.C.

Georgia O'Keeffe's brilliant poppy exalts structures that suggest erotic content in immaculate and simplified terms.

127 Spring Forms   *(illus.)*
By Loren MacIver (1909–)
1948. Oil on canvas, 26½ × 30¾
Courtesy Vassar College Art Gallery, Poughkeepsie, N.Y.

The delicacy in the figures in Loren MacIver's dark-toned canvases are refined and elegant. The economy of detail is romantic and imaginative.

128 American Painting   *(color, illus. p. 76)*
By Stuart Davis (1894–1964)
c. 1932–1950. Oil on canvas, 40 × 50
Courtesy Mrs. Stuart Davis, N.Y.C.

Davis was one of the painters of the thirties who worked in the WPA artists' project. National themes suited his beat—a syncopation of forms and colors. This composition, painted long after his time with the project, shows his special affinity for American themes and his skill in interpreting them.

129 South Wellfleet Inn   *(illus.)*
By Edwin Dickinson (1891–)
c. 1950. Oil on canvas, 33¼ × 43⅝
Courtesy Graham Galleries, N.Y.C.

The composition works back and forth between the painter's abstract vision and a realistic view of a landmark in a summer place that has long been a favorite of American artists.

130 The Subway   *(illus.)*
By George Tooker (1920–)
c. 1950. Egg tempera on composition board. 18⅛ × 36⅛
Courtesy Whitney Museum of American Art, N.Y.C.

Flight and fear are reiterated as this familiar urban setting becomes a nightmare maze of snares and traps.

131 The Brown Sweater   *(illus.)*
By Raphael Soyer (1899–)
c. 1952. Oil on canvas, 50 × 34
Courtesy Whitney Museum of American Art, N.Y.C.

Committing the commonplace to everlasting life is the intent of many of the American artists of social protest. This 1952 painting by Raphael Soyer is a late but particularly affecting example.

132 The Granddaughter   *(illus.)*
By Andrew Wyeth (1917–)
c. 1956. Oil on canvas, 23 × 17
Courtesy Mr. and Mrs. Robert Montgomery, N.Y.C.

Wyeth's genius in selecting and simplifying facts of personality and place is illustrated in these portraits of a Chadd's Ford neighbor, Alexander Chandler, and his young granddaughter.

133 Jura   *(illus.)*
   By Lee Gatch (1902–1968)
   c. 1961. Mixed media, 48 × 23½
   Courtesy Mr. and Mrs. Lee Ault, N.Y.C.

Architecture and anatomy are remembered in this beautifully ordered abstraction of a painting within a painting.

134 Locust in May
   By Charles Burchfield (1893–1967)
   c. 1965–1966. Oil on canvas, 46 × 30
   Courtesy Mr. and Mrs. Alfred Winslow Jones, N.Y.C.

Burchfield's ability to elevate the ordinary object to a level that makes the viewer reappraise its value is effectively demonstrated in this painting of trees in May.

135 The Rain Forest
   Three Botanical Studies
   By Joseph B. Martinson (1911–1970)
   1967–1970. Water color
   Courtesy Estate of Joseph B. Martinson

Most of his friends knew that one of the many talents of the late Joseph B. Martinson (whose memory this exhibition honors) was in sketching and painting. Although the artist was born and trained in New York this precise vision is of the rain forest that he saw from his home in Puerto Rico. The botanical studies are recent works that he was painting for an exhibition.

OPPOSITE: 47. *Kindred Spirits,* by Asher B. Durand

2. *Mrs. Petrus Vas* (Elsje Rutgers Schuyler Vas), by the de Peyster limner

3. *Pau de Wandelaer*, attributed to Pieter Vanderlyn

5. *Lapowinsa*, by Gustavus Hesselius

6. *Abraham Wendell*, by the Wendell limner

8. *Self Portrait at 24*, by Gilbert Stuart

7. *Joseph Sherburne*, by John Singleton Copley

9. *Dr. Philomen Tracy*, by an unidentified artist

10. *Elizabeth Tasker Lowndes* (Mrs. Christopher Lowndes), by Charles Willson Peale

13. *Sarah Prince*, by John Brewster, Jr.

14a. *Ephraim Starr*, by Simon Fitch

16. *Clarissa Partridge Childs*
(Mrs. Asa P. Childs), attributed to J. Brown

14b. *Hannah Beach Starr*, by Simon Fitch

18a. *General Schumacker's Daughter*,
by Jacob Maentel

18b. *General Schumacker*, by Jacob Maentel

20. *Elizabeth Fenimore Cooper*
(Mrs. William Cooper),
signed: Mr. Freeman

21. *The Shop and Warehouse of Duncan Phyfe*, by an unidentified artist

23. *View from Bluehill, Maine*, by Jonathan Fisher

24. *The Plantation*, by an unidentified artist

25. Scene from *The Last of the Mohicans*, by Thomas Cole

26. *View of Table Rock and Horseshoe Falls from Below,* by George Catlin

28. *The Peaceable Kingdom,* by Edward Hicks

31. *Ellen Tuttle Bangs*, by Erastus Salisbury Field

32. *Captain Smith of New London*, by Isaac Sheffield

34. *William Whipper*, by William Matthew Prior

36. *Self Portrait*, by Jonathan Fisher

37. *Ohio River Landscape*, by an unidentified artist

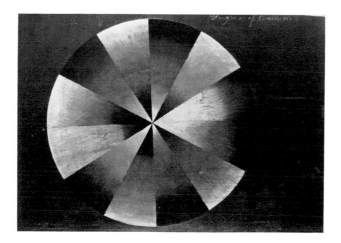

38. *Diagram of Contrasts*,
by Thomas Cole

39. *Political Banner*, by Terence Kennedy

43. *Cat in Open Window*, by an unidentified artist

54

44. *West Hartford Couple*, probably by Erastus S. Field

45. *The Residence of David Twining in 1785*, by Edward Hicks

49. *Sunnyside*, by George Inness

50. *Pavilion Beach*, *Gloucester*, by Fitz Hugh Lane

51. *Black Cat on a Chair*,
by Dr. Andrew L. von Wittcamp

56

52. *Reminiscences of the Catskill Mountains,*
by John Frederick Kensett

54. *Turkey Shoot,* by Tompkins H. Matteson

57. *War News from Mexico,*
     by Richard Caton Woodville

59. *Corn Husking*, by Eastman Johnson

58. *View of Sacramento, California,* by George Tirrell

60. *Bare Knuckles*, by George A. Hayes

61. *Wildflowers in a Glass Vase*, by an unidentified artist

62. *Mother and Son*, by William A. Walker

63. *After the Wedding in Warren, Pennsylvania,* by an unidentified artist

64. *General Doubleday Watching his Troops Cross the Potomac,* attributed to David Blythe

65. *Stag at Echo Rock*, by an
    unidentified artist

69. *Mount Whitney*, by Albert Bierstadt

70. *Salt Hay on the Rowley*,
by Martin Johnson Heade

72. *Barnegat Bay*,
by Francis Silva

73. *View of Benjamin
Reber's Farm*,
by Charles C. Hofmann

74. *John Biglen in a Single Scull*,
by Thomas Eakins

75. *The New Novel*,
by Winslow Homer

76. *Ballance Dry Dock*,
by Frederick Huge

63

78. *Old West Parlor*, by Ella Emery

80. *The Newsboy*, by George Newell Bowers

81. *The Morning Bell*, by Winslow Homer

79. *Harvest Moon*, by George Inness

82. *The Clock*, by John Haberle

85. *Trumpeter Swan*, by Alexander Pope

86. *Sportsman's Trophy*,
by Alexander Pope

66

87. *The Thinker*, by Thomas Eakins

89. *Club Night at Sharkey's*, by George Bellows

91. *Cinch Ring*, by Charles M. Russell

67

90. *Gold Panners' Camp—Big Horn Mountains, 1909,* by Frederick Remington

95. *Backyards, Greenwich Village*,
by John Sloan

98. *Manchester Valley*, by Joseph Pickett

100. *The Sale of Marblehead to the Indians for Eighty Dollars (1688)*, by J. O. J. Frost

102. *Bucks County Barn*, by Charles Sheeler

106. *Self Portrait*, by John Kane

107. *Woman with Plants*, by Grant Wood

110. *Mrs. Gamley*, by George Luks

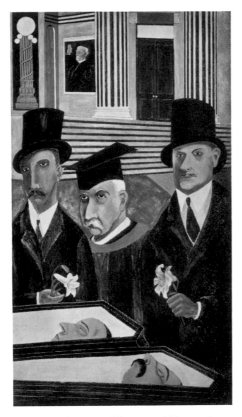

112. *The Passion of Sacco and Vanzetti,*
by Ben Shahn

114. *The Buffalo Hunt,* by Horace Pippin

117. *Early Sunday Morning,*
by Edward Hopper

72

118. *O, Chautauqua*, by Grant Wood

123. *Girl in Stars and Bars*, by Morris Hirschfield

122. *Fisherman's Last Supper*, by Marsden Hartley

124. *Seated Girl with Dog*, by Milton Avery

125. *Jimmy Savo and Rope*, by Adolf Dehn

74

126. *Poppy*, by Georgia O'Keeffe

127. *Spring Forms*, by Loren MacIver

128. *An American Painting*, by Stuart Davis

129. *South Wellfleet Inn*, by Edwin Dickerson

130. *The Subway*, by George Tooker

131. *The Brown Sweater,* by Raphael Soyer

132. *The Granddaughter,* by Andrew Wyeth

133. *Jura,* by Lee Gatch

Index

Italic page numbers indicate illustrations.